HABITAT
FACTS

by
William Anthony

BEARPORT
PUBLISHING

Minneapolis, Minnesota

Library of Congress Cataloging-in-Publication Data

Names: Anthony, William, 1996– author.
Title: Habitat facts / by William Anthony.
Description: Fusion books. | Minneapolis, Minnesota : Bearport
Publishing
Company, [2022] | Series: Fact-o-graphics! | Includes
bibliographical
references and index.
Identifiers: LCCN 2021005280 (print) | LCCN 2021005281 (ebook)
| ISBN
9781647479879 (library binding) | ISBN 9781647479923
(paperback) | ISBN
9781647479978 (ebook)
Subjects: LCSH: Habitat (Ecology)—Juvenile literature.
Classification: LCC QH541.14 .A58 2022 (print) | LCC QH541.14
(ebook) |
DDC 577—dc23
LC record available at https://lccn.loc.gov/2021005280
LC ebook record available at https://lccn.loc.gov/2021005281

For more information, write to Bearport Publishing, 5357 Penn
Avenue South, Minneapolis, MN 55419. Printed in the United
States of America.

Photo credits:
4 - Rvector, Lio putra, 5 - Beskova Ekaterina, practicuum, Tarikdiz, AnnstasAg, Tartila, 6 - Kirasolly, meunierd, A7880S, VectorsMarket,
7 - BorneoRimbawan, 8 - artbesouro, Molesko Studio, 9 - Vladislav T. Jirousek, Hennadii H, Ilyshev Dmitry, HappyPictures, Toltemara,
10 - KatePilko, Taras Dubov, K N, 11 - NPavelN, vfchen, Mr. Luck, 12 - Natali Snailcat, Dernkadel, VikiVector, fredrisher, Rvector, Caraulan Art,
Epica, 13 - MrVettore, Elena_sg80, Allexxandar, 14 - Andrei YUL, Spreadthesign, 15 - Giuseppe_R, nyker, Yakov Oskanov, 16 - Tarikdiz, Rhoeo,
Todd Boland, ArtDemidova, Jaaak, 17 - brgfx, lukpedclub, BSVIT, paradesign, gabigaasenbeek, BMJ, 18 - Jemastock, NotionPic, mauribo,
19 - A7880S, Waynerd, Watthano, 20 - mainfu, Ondrej Prosicky, 21 - Hanaha, Incomible, Rafael Martos Martins, Andrius Kaziliunas,
22 - Oliver Hoffmann, 23 - Tarikdiz.

Images are courtesy of Shutterstock.com. With thanks to Getty Images, Thinkstock Photo and iStockphoto.

CONTENTS

WHAT ARE HABITATS?

A habitat is a place where something lives. Deserts, mountains, and oceans are habitats.

Living things need food, water, **shelter**, space, and air in their habitats.

Air

Food

Shelter

Water

Space

Different animals have different ways of living in their habitats.

Polar bears live in cold habitats. They have thick fur to keep warm.

African elephants live in hot habitats. They flap their big ears to stay cool.

Cacti live in dry habitats. They hold water in their thick stems.

RAIN FORESTS

Rain forests are one kind of habitat. They have lots of rain and many tall trees. Rain forests are home to more than half of the plant and animal **species** on Earth!

Where Are Rain Forests?

■ Rain forests

Tapir

Many animals live in rain forests. There are tigers, monkeys, and tapirs!

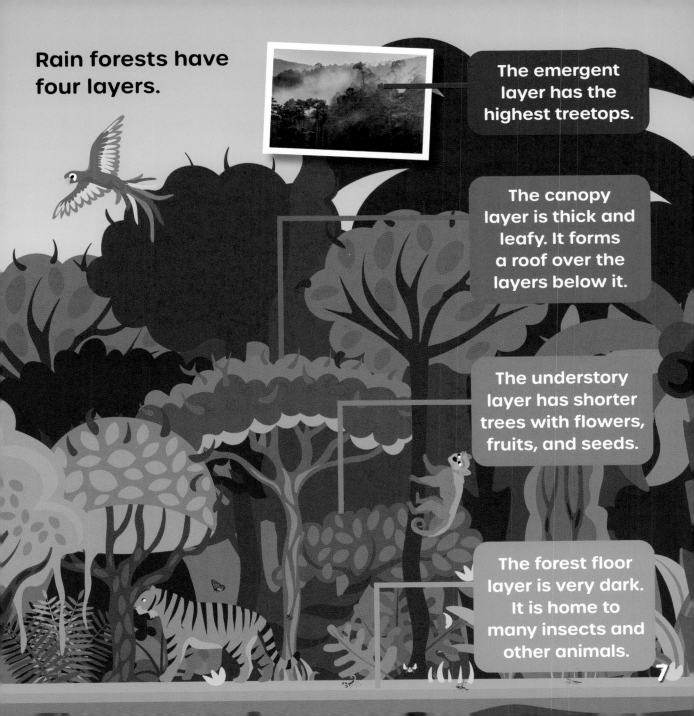

Rain forests have four layers.

The emergent layer has the highest treetops.

The canopy layer is thick and leafy. It forms a roof over the layers below it.

The understory layer has shorter trees with flowers, fruits, and seeds.

The forest floor layer is very dark. It is home to many insects and other animals.

DESERTS

A desert is a sandy and rocky habitat. Deserts are often very hot and have little water. Some do not get any rain for years!

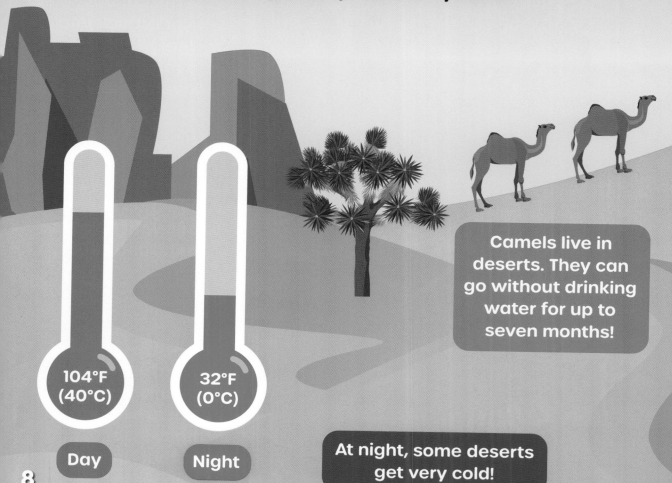

104°F
(40°C)

Day

32°F
(0°C)

Night

Camels live in deserts. They can go without drinking water for up to seven months!

At night, some deserts get very cold!

Desert animals such as foxes, turtles, rabbits, and rats get water from the food they eat.

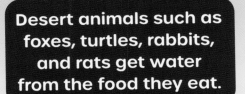

A cactus lives in a desert. This plant can hold water for a long time.

Some desert animals can beat the heat. The Cape ground squirrel uses its bushy tail to make its own shade.

9

COASTS

Coasts are habitats where the land meets the ocean. Coasts are always changing as ocean waves move rocks, sand, and even living things.

Cliffs

Sandy beaches

Rocky beaches

Some coasts have rocky beaches. Others have sandy beaches and cliffs.

Coasts are home to many kinds of **shellfish**, such as mussels. These shellfish stick to rocks so waves don't carry them away.

Shellfish can escape the waves but not the birds that eat them.

A seagull eating mussels

Mussels

OCEANS

Oceans are another kind of habitat. There are five oceans on Earth. A million kinds of plants and animals live in oceans. Scientists think there may be up to 9 million more species that we haven't found yet!

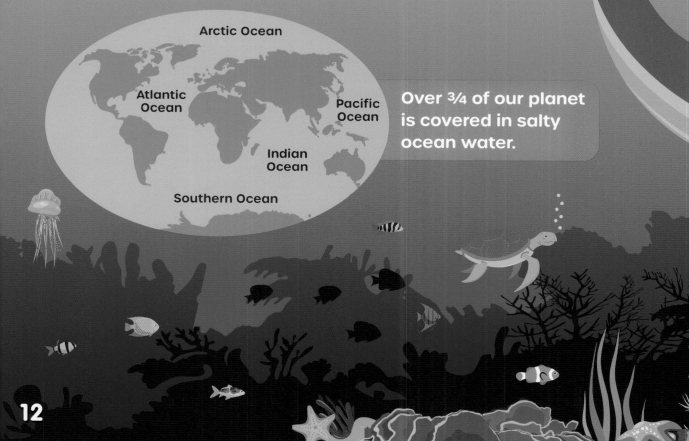

Arctic Ocean

Atlantic Ocean

Pacific Ocean

Indian Ocean

Southern Ocean

Over ¾ of our planet is covered in salty ocean water.

Many kinds of fish live in oceans. Whales, seahorses, and sea turtles live there, too.

The blue whale is the biggest animal in the world. It can be longer than two school buses!

The huge blue whale eats mostly tiny krill. It can eat 8 tons (7 metric tons) of krill a day!

Seahorse

Krill

GRASSLANDS

Grasslands are large, open areas of land. These habitats get more rain than deserts but less than rain forests. Grasslands are home to many kinds of animals, including antelopes, zebras, wolves, and buffalo.

Grasslands have wild oats, sunflowers, and purple coneflowers. These are all grasses!

Some of the biggest grassland **predators** include lions, cheetahs, and leopards.

Antelope

Meerkats dig **burrows** to hide from predators on grasslands. They take turns watching for danger from above.

MOUNTAINS

Mountains are habitats that rise high up toward the sky. A mountain is very different at the top, middle, and bottom.

Not many animals or plants live at the top of a mountain. This is because the air is very cold and is often hard to breathe.

Only small plants grow at the top of tall mountains.

Plants like these grow on rocks.

Mountain goats have hooves on their feet. They can walk up and down rocky mountains.

Mountain goat

Evergreen trees grow on lower parts of mountains. Their branches can hold lots of snow.

Lots of animals and forest plants live at the bottom of mountains, where it is warmer and easier to breathe.

Beaver

Grizzly bears can live on mountains, too. They sleep for most of the winter. This is called **hibernating**.

MICROHABITATS

Some very small animals have their own habitats inside bigger ones. These tiny homes are called microhabitats (mye-KROH-hab-i-tats).

Dragonflies live near ponds and lakes. Their babies live in pond microhabitats until they are fully grown.

Pond

A baby dragonfly under water

A baby owl lives in a hole in a tree. This microhabitat helps keep it safe.

Woodlice eat the microhabitat they live in! They live under logs and feed on the dead wood.

Logs and the undersides of rocks are microhabitats.

Rock

Log

DIFFERENT ADAPTATIONS

Animals and plants change to be able to live in their habitats. These changes are called adaptations. They happen over a long time.

Fish that live in the Arctic Ocean have adapted to the icy water.

The sword-billed hummingbird has a very long, thin beak. This lets it reach far inside flowers for food.

The silk floss tree has sharp spikes on its trunk. This stops animals from eating it.

The Texas horned lizard has a special trick to scare away predators. It shoots blood out of its eyes!

SAVING HABITATS

Humans cause a lot of **pollution**. This destroys habitats for plants and animals. But there are ways we can help.

The ice in cold habitats is melting. When people use lots of coal and oil, Earth heats up. Using less of these will help save habitats.

Driving a car pollutes the air. Walking or riding a bike is better for habitats.

Humans also destroy habitats by cutting down trees. Trees are used to make paper and other things. We can help save trees by **recycling**.

A piece of paper can be recycled up to seven times!

GLOSSARY

burrows holes or tunnels in the ground made by animals

hibernating going into a sleeplike state during periods of cold weather

pollution making the land, air, or water dirty and unsafe

predators animals that hunt other animals for food

recycling using something again to make something new

shellfish animals, such as crabs and lobsters, that have hard outer shells and live in water

shelter a place to live that provides food and safety

species groups of very similar animals or plants that can create young together

INDEX